THE NETHERLANDS

COUNTRY PROFILES

BY ALICIA Z. KLEPEIS

BELLWETHER MEDIA • MINNEAPOLIS, MN

Blastoff! Discovery launches a new mission: reading to learn. Filled with facts and features, each book offers you an exciting new world to explore!

This edition first published in 2020 by Bellwether Media, Inc.

No part of this publication may be reproduced in whole or in part without written permission of the publisher.
For information regarding permission, write to Bellwether Media, Inc., Attention: Permissions Department,
6012 Blue Circle Drive, Minnetonka, MN 55343.

Library of Congress Cataloging-in-Publication Data

Names: Klepeis, Alicia, 1971- author.
Title: The Netherlands / by Alicia Z. Klepeis.
Description: Minneapolis, MN : Bellwether Media, Inc., 2020. | Series: Blastoff! Discovery: Country Profiles | Includes bibliographical references and index. | Audience: Ages 7-13.
Identifiers: LCCN 2019001506 (print) | LCCN 2019002133 (ebook) | ISBN 9781618915924 (ebook) | ISBN 9781644870518 (hardcover : alk. paper)
Subjects: LCSH: Netherlands–Juvenile literature
Classification: LCC DJ18 (ebook) | LCC DJ18 .K54 2020 (print) | DDC 949.2–dc23
LC record available at https://lccn.loc.gov/2019001506

Text copyright © 2020 by Bellwether Media, Inc. BLASTOFF! DISCOVERY and associated logos are trademarks and/or registered trademarks of Bellwether Media, Inc. SCHOLASTIC, CHILDREN'S PRESS, and associated logos are trademarks and/or registered trademarks of Scholastic Inc., 557 Broadway, New York, NY 10012.

Editor: Rebecca Sabelko   Designer: Brittany McIntosh

Printed in the United States of America, North Mankato, MN.

TABLE OF CONTENTS

BOATS AND BIKES	4
LOCATION	6
LANDSCAPE AND CLIMATE	8
WILDLIFE	10
PEOPLE	12
COMMUNITIES	14
CUSTOMS	16
SCHOOL AND WORK	18
PLAY	20
FOOD	22
CELEBRATIONS	24
TIMELINE	26
THE NETHERLANDS FACTS	28
GLOSSARY	30
TO LEARN MORE	31
INDEX	32

BOATS AND BIKES

THE ROYAL PALACE
AMSTERDAM

On a bright spring morning, a family arrives in Amsterdam. They rent bicycles and cruise around the city like the locals. They pass by blooming fruit trees and flowers and tall, colorful **terraced** houses. They stop at a sidewalk café and enjoy a light meal and pastries.

OTHER TOP SITES

DELFT TOWN HALL

DUNES OF TEXEL NATIONAL PARK

KEUKENHOF GARDENS

WINDMILLS AT KINDERDIJK

After lunch, the family pedals on to visit the Royal Palace. This amazing building is decorated with marble sculptures and huge paintings. In the early evening, the family boards a **canal** boat. They have a delicious meal while cruising along the city's many canals. Welcome to the Netherlands!

LOCATION

The Netherlands is located in western Europe. It covers 16,040 square miles (41,543 square kilometers). The capital, Amsterdam, lies in the western part of the country. The waters of the North Sea make up the Netherlands' western and northern borders. Belgium lies to the south. Germany is the Netherlands' eastern neighbor.

Most of the Netherlands' land is in Europe. But the nation's **territory** also includes the Caribbean islands of Bonaire, Saba, and St. Eustatius. The **Kingdom** of the Netherlands also includes the three Caribbean countries of Aruba, Curaçao, and St. Maarten.

NORTH SEA

LANDSCAPE AND CLIMATE

The Netherlands is one of the world's flattest countries. About half of the nation is less than a few feet above sea level. The North Sea would have washed much of the nation's land away if people had not built dams, canals, and **dikes** to protect it. **Polders** are found along the coast.

FROM SEA TO LAKE

The biggest lake in the Netherlands is the IJsselmeer. It started as a part of the North Sea called the Zuiderzee but was dammed to become a lake. Over time, the IJsselmeer switched from seawater to fresh water!

IJSSELMEER

POLDER

AMSTERDAM
Average seasonal highs and lows

JANUARY
HIGH: 42 °F (6 °C)
LOW: 33 °F (1 °C)

APRIL
HIGH: 55 °F (13 °C)
LOW: 40 °F (4 °C)

JULY
HIGH: 71 °F (22 °C)
LOW: 55 °F (13 °C)

OCTOBER
HIGH: 58 °F (14 °C)
LOW: 45 °F (7 °C)

°F = degrees Fahrenheit
°C = degrees Celsius

The low rolling hills in the center of the country get taller as they stretch southeastward. Several rivers flow through the Netherlands, including the Rhine, the Scheldt, and the Maas.

Thanks to its location by the sea, the Netherlands has a **temperate** climate. Summers are cool and winters are mild.

WILDLIFE

The Netherlands is quite crowded with people so animals have to make their homes around the canals, dikes, and dams. The nation's 20 national parks also provide great **habitats** for wildlife. Beavers swim and deer graze in the marshy forests and grasslands of De Biesbosch National Park. Kingfishers and eagles soar overhead. Pine martens chase their prey through the trees.

Badgers play amidst the sand dunes in De Loonse en Drunense Duinen National Park. In the waters off the coast of the North Sea, porpoises feed on smaller fish like gobies as crabs and lobsters crawl about below.

EURASIAN BEAVER

HARBOUR PORPOISE

EUROPEAN BADGER

THE BISON ARE BACK

Bison were hunted to extinction in Europe in the early 1900s. But they have been reintroduced into the wild in the Netherlands. Today, a herd lives on the sand dunes of Kraansvlak in the northern region of Holland.

PEOPLE

More than 17 million people call the Netherlands home. Most of the nation's people are Dutch. People from different nations in the **European Union** (EU) make up the second-largest group. Other people have **emigrated** from countries such as Turkey, Morocco, and Indonesia. Many Dutch live in the Randstad region in the western Netherlands, which includes several cities.

About half of the people in the Netherlands do not follow any religion. Of those who do, most are Christian. Some are Roman Catholic, while others are Protestant. Dutch is the only official language of the Netherlands. One exception is in the Friesland **province** where Frisian is the official language.

FAMOUS FACE

Name: Ireen Wüst
Birthday: April 1, 1986
Hometown: Goirle, Netherlands
Famous for: The Netherlands' most successful Olympic athlete and the winner of 11 medals in speed skating

SPEAK DUTCH

ENGLISH	DUTCH	HOW TO SAY IT
hello	hallo	HAH low
goodbye	tot ziens	toht zeens
please	alstublieft	ahls-tew-BLEEFT
thank you	dank u	DAHNK ew
yes	ja	YAA
no	nee	NAY

AMSTERDAM

COMMUNITIES

Most Dutch live in **urban** areas. Terraced houses with front and back gardens are a common sight in many neighborhoods. These homes are often two or three stories tall. In big cities like Amsterdam, most people live in apartments. It is very common to travel by bike. There are also buses, trains, trams, and even ferries. **Rural** homes are often made of bricks. People in the countryside use bikes and cars to get around.

BICYCLES EVERYWHERE

The Netherlands has more bicycles than residents. In fact, the Dutch own more bikes per person than any other country on earth! Amsterdam has even been called "the bicycle capital of the world."

Families in the Netherlands are small, often with one or two children. Both parents take an active role in raising children. Since both parents commonly work outside the home, grandparents help raise children, too.

CUSTOMS

Since it is often gray and dreary outside, people in the Netherlands do not miss any chance to get into the sun. Sometimes this means calling in sick on a workday. Other times, the Dutch will leave the office early when the sky is bright. Sun lovers can be seen in city centers across the country soaking in the rays.

Even though it is not common to just drop by for an unannounced visit, the Dutch enjoy hosting visitors. They often offer guests coffee or tea and sweets such as cookies. Dinner guests typically bring flowers and wine to their host's home.

WOODEN SHOES

The Netherlands is famous for its wooden clogs or shoes, known as *klompen*. Most are sold to tourists today. But every June, a baseball game is played in the Hague where all players wear klompen.

SCHOOL AND WORK

Students in the Netherlands must begin school at age 5, though many attend preschool first. Primary education is required through age 12. Students attend secondary school for another four to six years. Some secondary pupils get ready for college. Others train for a specific profession. The Netherlands has several universities for students who have completed secondary school.

Most workers in the Netherlands have **service jobs**. They might work in the government, health care, or education fields. Other Dutch people **manufacture** products like machinery, medical equipment, and vehicles. Farmers raise livestock, grow vegetables, and produce dairy products.

VEHICLE MANUFACTURING

TONS OF TULIPS

The Netherlands is the world's largest producer of tulip bulbs. Each year the nation produces more than 4 billion bulbs. Some of the colorful tulip fields can even be seen from space!

PLAY

SOCCER STAR

In 2017, a Dutch citizen named Lieke Martens was voted the world's best women's soccer player. She has played professionally in Belgium, Germany, Sweden, and Spain.

The Dutch enjoy sports all year round. Soccer is the country's most popular sport. Swimming, sailing, and waterskiing are common activities during the summer months. In the winter, many Dutch enjoy ice skating. Most towns in the Netherlands have their own outdoor skating rinks. When the weather is cold enough, people will skate along the nation's frozen canals.

ICE SKATING

Families in the Netherlands often take weekend trips or longer vacations in summer. Camping is a popular activity, as are bicycle vacations. Some folks go on hiking trips as well. Skiing is popular during the winter.

BICYCLE TRIP

DELFT POTTERY

The city of Delft is famous for its blue-and-white pottery, which often features landscape scenes or images of daily life in the Netherlands.

What You Need:
- white paper plates
- pencil
- blue markers, colored pencils, or paint

Instructions:
1. Spend a little time looking at images of Delft pottery so you are familiar with its style.
2. On your paper plate, sketch your design with a pencil.
3. Use your marker, pencil, or paint to create your white-and-blue design.
4. If using paint, let it dry completely. Otherwise, put your creation on display for all to see!

FOOD

TASTY TREATS

Desserts come in many forms in the Netherlands. *Stroopwafels* are thin waffles or wafers with a caramel-like filling. *Vla* is a sweet pudding. The Dutch are also famous for their salty licorice!

It is common for the Dutch to start their day with coffee or tea and bread. Some people have butter or cheese with the bread. Others prefer chocolate spread or even chocolate sprinkles, known as *hagelslag*! Lunch might be an open-faced sandwich. One popular variety includes sliced ham or roast beef with fried eggs. Sandwiches might be served with vegetable soup, or *groentesoep*.

Potatoes are a **staple** in the Dutch diet. People eat a lot of seafood in the Netherlands, too. Eel and herring are favorites. Indonesian food is well-liked, with its many spices and flavors.

HAGELSLAG

GROENTESOEP

CHOCOLATE VLA

Chocolate *vla* is a popular Dutch dessert. Try this easy recipe with the help of an adult!

Ingredients:
2 cups milk
3 tablespoons plus 1 teaspoon cornstarch
5 tablespoons unsweetened cocoa powder
4 tablespoons sugar

Steps:
1. In a bowl, whisk together the cornstarch, cocoa powder, and sugar until well mixed.
2. Add 1/2 cup of milk to this dry mixture and whisk again until it is like a paste.
3. Place a saucepan on the stove and bring the remaining 1 1/2 cups of milk to a boil. Gradually add the cocoa mixture while whisking this on the stove. The pudding should thicken within a minute or so.
4. Turn down the heat and stir the mixture for two minutes while it simmers.
5. Take off the heat and pour the pudding into a bowl. Cover it with plastic wrap.
6. Let the mixture cool in the refrigerator and then serve.

CELEBRATIONS

Some celebrations in the Netherlands are Christian holidays. Carnival takes place during the three days leading up to Lent. Many Dutch cities hold parades during this time. Music plays and people dance while wearing colorful costumes. The feast of St. Nicholas is on December 5. Kids put their shoes by the fireplace hoping to receive a surprise.

April 27 is King Willem-Alexander's birthday. It is also a public holiday. Across the country, people celebrate with parties, concerts, and street markets. Many wear orange, which is the national color. But the Dutch celebrate their country and **culture** throughout the year!

THE HOLLAND FESTIVAL

The Holland Festival is an exciting time in Amsterdam. Occurring in June, the festival involves concerts, plays, ballet performances, and more.

TIMELINE

1568
Prince William of Orange leads a revolt against Spanish rule, kicking off the Eighty Years' War

AROUND 50 CE
Roman settlements are established

1602
The Dutch East India Company is established to support the Dutch war of independence from Spain

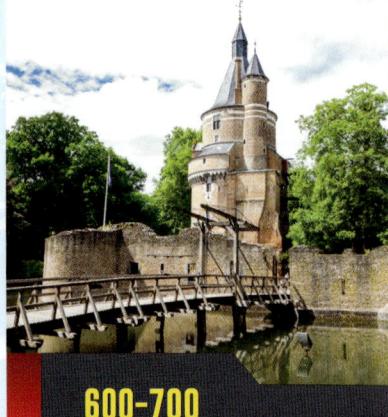

600-700
Dorestad becomes an important center for trade

1600-1690
Immigrants flood to Amsterdam for safety bringing creativity and influence which begins a period called the Golden Age

1648
The Eighty Years' War ends and Spain recognizes Dutch independence

2013
King Willem-Alexander takes the throne, replacing Queen Beatrix and becoming the first king in over a century

2001
The Netherlands becomes the first country to legalize same-sex marriages

1940-1945
Nazi Germany occupies the Netherlands during World War II

2018
A law is drafted to ban using cell phones while on bicycles

THE NETHERLANDS FACTS

Official Name: Kingdom of the Netherlands

Flag of The Netherlands: The Netherlands' flag has three horizontal bands of color. The top band is red, the center band is white, and the bottom band is blue. Originally the top band was orange, but its dye turned red over time. It was permanently changed to red. The colors were taken from those of William I, Prince of Orange. He was in charge of the Dutch revolt against Spanish rule.

Area: 16,040 square miles (41,543 square kilometers)

Capital City: Amsterdam

Important Cities: Rotterdam, The Hague, Utrecht

Population: 17,151,228 (July 2018)

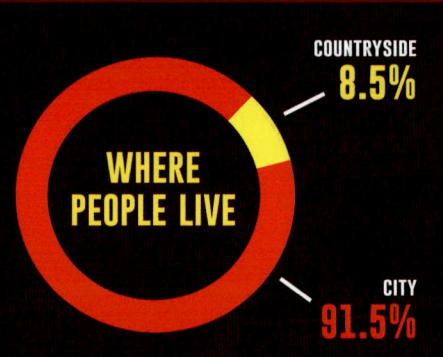

WHERE PEOPLE LIVE

COUNTRYSIDE 8.5%

CITY 91.5%

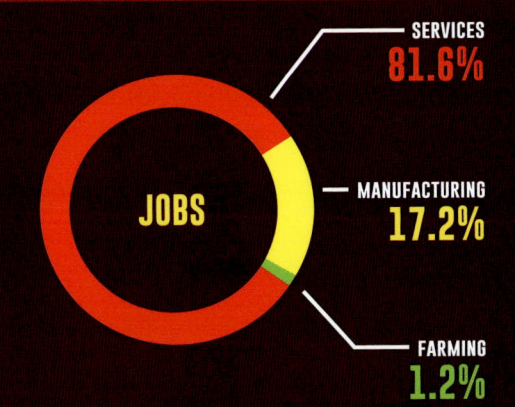

Main Exports:

machinery   chemicals   flowers

transport equipment   mineral fuels   food and livestock

National Holidays:
King's Day (April 27), Liberation Day (May 5)

Main Languages:
Dutch, Frisian (Friesland province)

Form of Government:
parliamentary constitutional monarchy

Title for Country Leaders:
king (head of state); prime minister (head of government)

Unit of Money:
euro

29

GLOSSARY

canal—related to a waterway for boats

culture—the beliefs, arts, and ways of life in a place or society

dikes—banks of dirt built to control water

emigrated—left a country or region to move to another country

European Union—a group of 27 European countries with many shared laws and rights; all EU countries use the euro.

habitats—lands with certain types of plants, animals, and weather

kingdom—a country which has a king or queen as its ruler

manufacture—to make products, often with machines

polders—large pieces of low-lying land that have been reclaimed from the sea

province—an area within a country; provinces follow all the laws of the country and make some of their own laws.

rural—related to the countryside

service jobs—jobs that perform tasks for people or businesses

staple—a widely used food or other item

temperate—associated with a mild climate that does not have extreme heat or cold

terraced—referring to homes that are similar in style and share their side walls

territory—a geographic area which belongs to a government

urban—related to cities and city life

TO LEARN MORE

AT THE LIBRARY

Drummond, Allan. *Pedal Power: How One Community Became the Bicycle Capital of the World*. New York, N.Y.: Farrar, Straus and Giroux, 2017.

Hintz, Martin. *The Netherlands*. New York, N.Y.: Children's Press, 2016.

Murray, Julie. *Netherlands*. Minneapolis, Minn.: Big Buddy Books, 2018.

ON THE WEB

FACTSURFER

Factsurfer.com gives you a safe, fun way to find more information.

1. Go to www.factsurfer.com.

2. Enter "The Netherlands" into the search box and click 🔍.

3. Select your book cover to see a list

INDEX

activities, 4, 5, 20, 21
Amsterdam, 4-5, 6, 7, 9, 13, 14, 15, 24
capital (see Amsterdam)
Carnival, 24, 25
celebrations, 24-25
climate, 9, 16, 20
communities, 14-15
customs, 16-17
Delft pottery (activity), 21
education, 18, 19
fast facts, 28-29
feast of St. Nicholas, 24
food, 4, 17, 22-23
Holland Festival, 24
housing, 4, 14
King Willem-Alexander's birthday, 24
kingdom, 6
landmarks, 5
landscape, 8-9, 10
language, 13
Lent, 24
location, 6-7
Martens, Lieke, 20

people, 12-13
recipe, 23
religion, 13, 24
Royal Palace, 4, 5
size, 6
sports, 17, 20, 21
territories, 6
timeline, 26-27
transportation, 4, 5, 14, 15
wildlife, 10-11
work, 16, 18, 19
Wüst, Ireen, 13

The images in this book are reproduced through the courtesy of: Travelerpix, cover; V_E, pp. 4-5; S-F, pp. 5 (top), 9 (right); Eric Valenne geostory, p. 5 (top middle); Neirfy, p. 5 (bottom middle); SergiyN, p. 5 (bottom); AridOcean, pp. 6-7, 8 (top); Cyrille Gibot/ Getty, p. 8; Harry Beugelink, p. 9; Vaclav Sebek, p. 10 (left); Podolnaya Elena, p. 10 (top); Elise V, p. 10 (middle); Randy van Domselaar, p. 10 (bottom); Milan Zygmunt, p. 11; Mila Supinskaya Glashchenko, p. 12; CTK/ Alamy, p. 13 (top); lornet, pp. 13, 15; Jan Wlodarczyk, p. 14; fokke baarssen, p. 16; marek kasula/ Alamy, p. 17; photo one, p. 17 (shoes); ton koene/ Alamy, pp. 18, 19 (top), 19; Vincent Jannink/ Newscom, p. 20; Steve Photography, p. 20; Ferry Beekes/ Alamy, p. 21 (top); MyImages-Micha, p. 21; jan kranendonk, p. 22; Poleijphoto, p. 23 (top); Joshua Rainey Photography, p. 23 (middle); larik_malasha, p. 23 (bottom); Celli07, p. 24; NurPhoto/ Getty, p. 25; TasfotoNL, p. 26; Marcel Alsemgees, p. 27; thodonal88, p. 29 (left); Andrey Lobachev, p. 29 (right).